WS

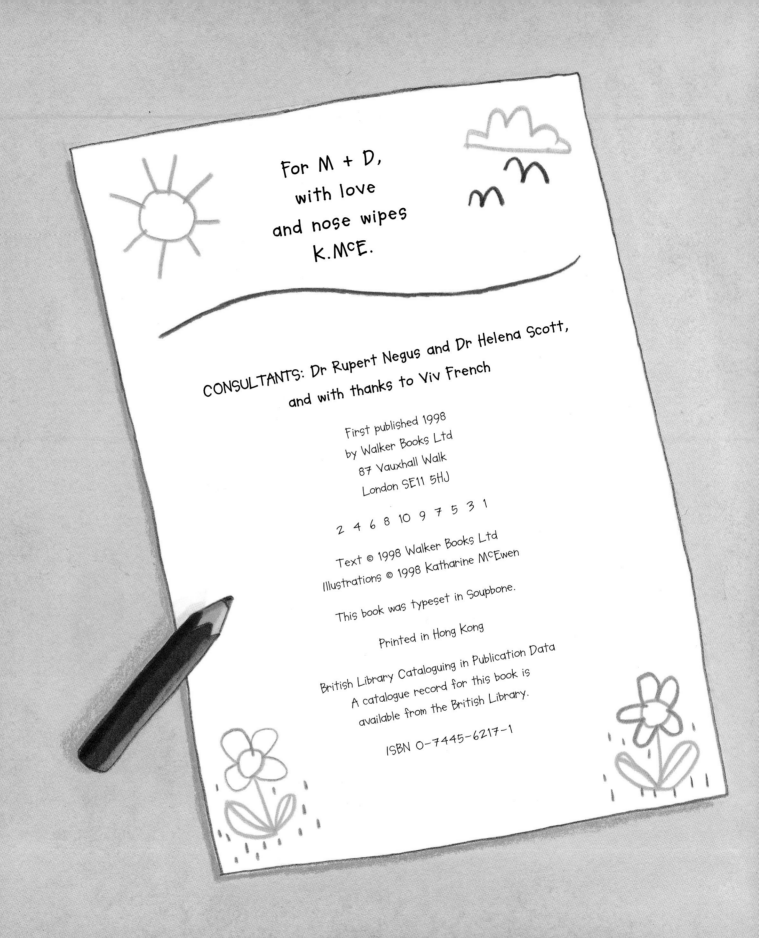

For M + D,
with love
and nose wipes
K.McE.

CONSULTANTS: Dr Rupert Negus and Dr Helena Scott,
and with thanks to Viv French

First published 1998
by Walker Books Ltd
87 Vauxhall Walk
London SE11 5HJ

2 4 6 8 10 9 7 5 3 1

Text © 1998 Walker Books Ltd
Illustrations © 1998 Katharine McEwen

This book was typeset in Soupbone.

Printed in Hong Kong

British Library Cataloguing in Publication Data
A catalogue record for this book is
available from the British Library.

ISBN 0-7445-6217-1

I KNOW HOW WE FIGHT GERMS

KATE ROWAN

illustrated by

KATHARINE McEwen

WALKER BOOKS
AND SUBSIDIARIES
LONDON • BOSTON • SYDNEY

"ATCHOOOOO!"

Sam sneezed

an enormous sneeze.

"Sam!" said Mum.
"That's DISGUSTING!
Haven't you got a tissue?"
And she pulled one out of her
pocket and wiped his nose.

"Thanks," said Sam,
and he sneezed again.
"ATCHOOOOO!"

"You've got a cold,"
said Mum.

"I know," said Sam, "and I know why colds make me sneeze. When I sneeze I'm blowing cold germs out of my body."

sneeze

"You certainly are," said Mum. "That's how cold germs spread to other people, and why you need to catch your sneeze in a tissue. If someone else breathes your cold germs in, they might get a cold, too."

8

"Oh," said Sam.
"Is that how
I got this
cold then?"

"Probably," said Mum.
"I expect you caught it
       from someone at school."

ATCHOOO!

"We did germs at school," said Sam.

"My teacher said you can sneeze them
a really long way. She said you can sneeze
them as far as 10 metres."

"That IS a long way," said Mum.

"That's as far as three elephants standing in a line!"

Sam giggled. "I wouldn't like to be near an elephant when it sneezed!"

"ATCHOOOOO!"
Sam peered
at his tissue.
"You can't see
germs, can you?"

"No," said Mum, "they're too tiny. Even the biggest ones are so small you could fit hundreds of thousands of them on top of your thumb. You can only see germs if you look at them under a microscope."

microscope

Sam sniffed.

"I bet I've got MILLIONS of germs inside me."

"BILLIONS!" said Mum. "But not all germs make us ill, and when they do, our bodies try to fight them off."

"I know," said Sam.

"I've got something in
my blood that fights germs."

14

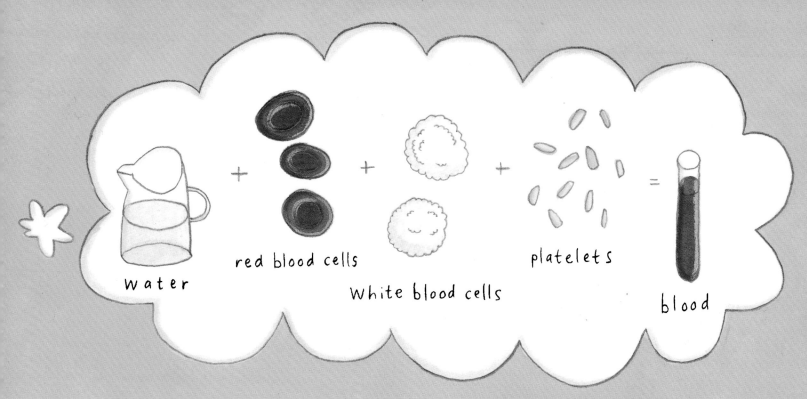

water   red blood cells   white blood cells   platelets   blood

"That's right," said Mum.
"About half your blood is water,
but there are also lots of things
in it called **cells** — red ones and
white ones. And there are bits
of **cells** called **platelets**, too."

"Are there?" asked Sam.
"Is that why blood
is red — 'cos of
the **red blood cells**?"

Mum nodded.

"And the **white blood cells** are
the ones that kill off the germs.
They make special chemicals,
then they zap the cold
germs with the chemicals
and kill them."

"Cool," said Sam.

"Germ busters to the rescue!"

And he sneezed again.

chickenpox germ

"You'd better put your coat on," said Mum. "Keeping warm helps your body fight colds."

"OK," said Sam. "But cold germs aren't the only bad germs, are they? 'Cos when I had chickenpox the doctor said I'd got chickenpox germs."

"So he did," said Mum.
"That's because there are lots of
different germs. They all do different
things, and scientists sort them
out into groups. One group is
called **viruses** — cold germs
and chickenpox germs
are both **viruses**."

19

"Oh yeah, I remember," said Sam.
"There are some germs called
bac... something, too."

"Bacteria," said Mum.
"They're another germ group.
Bacteria live on all kinds of
things, but they especially love dirt.
So if you eat dirty food or don't wash
your hands before meals, bad bacteria
can get into your body."

Sam wiped his nose.
"Do white blood cells zap
the bac things, too, then?"

"They do kill them, but not by zapping," said Mum.

"When bad **bacteria** get into your blood, the **white blood cells** come along and gobble them up!"

"GROSS!" said Sam.

"Germ munchers to the rescue!"

21

"How do you know about **bacteria** anyway?" asked Mum.

Sam showed her the scab on his elbow.

"When I fell over at school, my teacher washed the dirt off and put some stingy cream on the cut. She said it was for the bac stuff."

"Bacteria," said Mum.

"Yeah," said Sam, "she said they might get into the cut. The cream helps to kill them, and then a scab grows to keep them out. She said scabs are made by my blood going all sticky and hard."

"That's where the **platelets** come in," explained Mum, "the bits of **cells** I was telling you about. Scabs are made by billions of **platelets** and **red blood cells** clumping and lumping together."

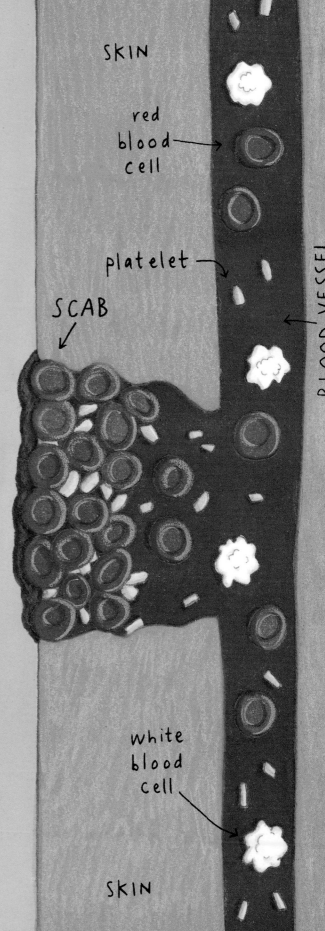

SKIN

red blood cell

platelet

BLOOD VESSEL

SCAB

white blood cell

SKIN

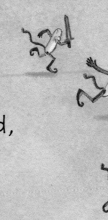

"Yeah," said Sam.
"And when the skin's mended,
the scab falls off."

"And that's why you need to keep
cuts clean and not pick at scabs
before they're ready to come
off by themselves," said Mum,
"so the bad **bacteria**
don't get in."

"I know," said Sam.
"But I LIKE picking
at scabs."

CASTLE ELBOW

25

"Not all **bacteria** are bad, though," said Mum. "You've got good **bacteria** living inside you all the time, helping to keep you healthy. And some food has good **bacteria** in it, too — like yoghurt and cheese. There are even **bacteria** that help to make good soil."

"Have we got good soil?"
asked Sam.

"Yes," said Mum.
"That's why we
grow such great
vegetables!"

Sam sighed.

"Like spinach, you mean."

She sneezed an enormous sneeze.

"Mum!" said Sam.

"That's DISGUSTING!

Haven't you got a tissue?"